I0004196

Cover by Brandi McCann at www.ebook-coverdesigns.com

Copyright © 2015 Cory Berg

All rights reserved.

To Deb, for reviewing my work and being patient during the many hours I spent writing this.

To John and Allen, for looking at my early revision, being polite in spite of it, and questioning my assumptions.

To Michael, Todd, and Alekhya, and everyone who reviewed this before I finally called it Done, thank you.

And finally, to all my colleagues that helped shape my own direction in one form or another.
You know who you are.

Introduction

This book is for any junior or mid-level professional involved in a technical craft who is looking to improve his or her non-technical skills in a corporate context. In this book, I offer you some advice and perspective that I have gained throughout my years in the software industry, based on real situations (and real mistakes) of my own personal experience. These are skills that I wish I had learned twenty years ago. These are "must-have" skills, in the sense that mastering them will help you to operate more effectively within the technical realm and far beyond that realm. With each "must-have," I include exercises that you can use to underline the point for yourself. At the core, this is all about your awareness and your diligence. Once you are aware of your strengths, your weaknesses, and the environment around you, you can start to experiment with these variables, and possibly influence outcomes for yourself, your life, and your career direction.

Throughout my entire adult life I have been an engineer, focused on software as a deliverable. Professionally, I have never done anything else. I have worked with some of the largest companies in the world, and I have worked with startups that were less than twenty strong. I started out building military and FAA software products – the sort where "mission critical" meant that actual lives were at stake. My introduction to "real" software engineering was less than spectacular – I remember getting harshly and deservedly abused on my first peer-to-peer code review. Those lessons translated into increased discipline in my own practices. I was lucky enough to have experienced colleagues around who guided me along the way, sometimes in positive ways and sometimes in negative ways. I decided that the best way to honor those people is to share some of the more important lessons with you.

Before we go further, I would like to address a couple important points of terminology.

Terminology: Strategic and Tactical

The words *"strategic"* and *"tactical"* come from the military, but they are valuable words as a basis for classifying certain elements of the corporate world. If you are just starting out in your software career, you are probably focused on tactical concerns: the coding, the product, and the immediate, short-term deliveries. You are expected to apply your technical skill directly to the job at hand. Strategic work, on the other hand, involves a broader perspective, thinking in larger scopes and higher levels of abstraction, often involving longer time frames. In your software life, you may experience an evolution of your company. Most companies start out as very tactically-oriented. They rely on the short-term skills, creativity, and fast time to market; the goals are to build revenue, capitalize on opportunities, and so forth. If they are successful, such companies evolve into more strategic focus - certainly they still deliver product, but it is with consideration of a longer-term plan. Similarly, your software career might evolve as well. You may choose to move from a skilled technical role, to a more abstract, broad-thinking operator with a big-picture focus. My point: you should recognize that there are tactical concerns, and there are strategic concerns, and these things are often regarded, used, analyzed, and executed very differently. Moving from tactical concerns to strategic concerns (and vice-versa) can be very challenging, and the same can be said for moving from a company at one level to a company at another. The good news is this: your basis in technical capability can serve you well in either capacity.

Terminology: Engineers, Developers, and Programmers

The software industry has some interesting challenges that set it apart from classic engineering disciplines. There has always been debate about the use of terminology between the terms "software engineer," "software developer" and "programmer" (among other terms.) In this book, I will generally use the word "engineer" because I am an engineer. Historically, the addition of the word "engineer" implied a certain degree of professional behavior, capability, and often liability. But, while I have an engineering degree, some of the best software people I have worked with do not. So, for the purposes of this book, I will set aside the debates and start from the basis that we are in the technical realm because we enjoy the work. The fact that you are reading this book implies that you are embarking on your own journey to hone your skills and expand your horizons. There is nothing more "engineering" than that.

Organization of this Book

This book is arranged in three parts. The first part is about you and your own skills. The second part is about how you relate to your colleagues. The third part is about your place within an organization – which could be the company you work for, a trade association, and so on. This arrangement is deliberate; it is based on the philosophy that if you understand yourself, then you are in a better position to understand others – something I have found to be a truism, however challenging at times. You don't have to read this book from front to back, like a novel; you may come back to it from time to time and see a slightly different interpretation, depending on where you are in your career.

Let's get started!

Part I: About You

Skill #1: Always Have a Definition of Done

Within most organizations, engineers are part of the team that builds the product, service, structures, et cetera. As such, the number one priority of the engineer is **to deliver on objectives**. If you take the job seriously, you need to make sure you do this. However, to do it successfully, you must understand the "Definition of Done" for your specific situation.

The Definition of Done refers to the set of conditions that define a successful end result. These conditions are the criteria by which you determine when your project is "finished." Strangely enough, these success criteria are often unclear, ill-defined, or assumed to be obvious at the risk of going totally unidentified. Indeed, projects can have huge numbers of well-written requirements, and still result in dismal failure because nobody considered what it meant to be successful. So, the Definition of Done is not the same as the precision of your project requirements. The actual Definition of Done can take many different forms, and it can change as your project evolves. At some companies, the Definition of Done is nicely captured in the form of a product management-level "market requirements" document. On the other extreme, it is left as a set of assumptions that might not be communicated to the development side of the organization.

My personal preference for expressing a Definition of Done is to formulate a simple set of direct, high-level statements that are agreed between business and technical teams. This set of statements becomes a deliverable set of "assumptions" in the same manner as the requirements themselves. This is best agreed upon early in the process, but it sometimes happens mid-stream. As a real-world example, imagine that you are in your second last iteration of a project, and you thought you knew the expectations for "go-live" - one month for final integration testing, and a nice gradual ramp-up of new customers. Then the business says "Change of plan, we are going to sign up 50,000 customers in the first week, and take two weeks away from that integration testing." Did the functional requirements change? No, although one could argue that the non-functional requirements - if they were captured - changed. But the Definition of Done for this phase of development has certainly been modified. You had better put some emphasis on performance and scalability now, even if that means trading off the last bits of functionality in your last iteration. By extension, this means you should have a direct, open, honest conversation with your business colleagues, because they are probably going to have to make some tough compromises on functionality. That conversation should result in a modified Definition of Done that is written and socialized to the key stakeholders.

The more specifically you can call out the Definition of Done, the more tangible your end goal will be, and the greater your likelihood of success. For example:

- Does "done" equal a software product that performs well and looks nice, but is so complex to maintain, that it drives the company out of business? Probably not!
- Does "done" equal a small operational piece of a larger product that a real customer will use?
- Is "done" really a prototype that should go no further than the prototype stage?
- Is it possible to achieve a specific technical definition of "done?"

Exercise: When you are scoping your next project, have a brainstorming session on what "done" actually means for that project. You might find yourself adjusting your strategy right at the start, which is far less expensive than adjusting it later.

Real-World Tale: I once inherited a project that was about six months into development. After one particularly important operational demo, I asked for feedback from the sponsoring business VP. The VP's response was simply: "I don't love it." Although an emotionally-rooted statement, it was a simple and honest observation from the VP's standpoint. However, from my perspective, this *informal opinion revealed that the previously understood Definition of Done was possibly more subjective than I had considered.   With this realization, I reconsidered the Definition of Done, together with the VP and the business organization. This in turn established that the VP was in fact overriding the product owner's decisions; this led to a modified requirements process that more closely involved the VP's point of view.   If I were not paying attention to what I understood as the Definition of Done, I might have ignored the significance of the comment, and I may have been surprised to later find that the product was not acceptable to the business leadership - but by then it would have been too late.*

It is ironic that the Definition of Done is nearly always a key conversation for a software development contract, since there is explicit money tied to completion milestones.   Yet for many in-house projects, it is common to start coding without even considering the criteria for success, even though there is still money funding the effort. I take great pains to employ this thinking every time I do a discrete piece of work.   In some cases, the evaluation of the Definition of Done can (rightly so, I think) stop an entire project while the team adjusts its scope based on the revised success criteria. If you want to add real value to your team and to your own perspective as you grow into a senior engineer, pay attention to the Definition of Done.

Skill #2: Reason From Facts

As analytical people, we engineers often associate our ego with our work. But this brings some potential negative side effects:

- The desire to be "correct" causes us to attach our ego to the very argument we make for our own correctness.
- When the ego is involved, we will sometimes make up our minds on a certain solution or approach, even if facts point to the contrary.

Both of these items means we are easily hurt when our ideas are challenged, resulting in a defensive position. What would happen if you made up your mind, then were proven 100% wrong? Would it be difficult to back down from your position on the topic? Approaching discussions from a fact-based perspective can help reduce or eliminate the feeling of being attached to one's position. If the facts change, your position may need to change in response.

Many top software engineers share two key attributes in this regard:

- They focus on facts rather than emotion-based positions. It is no coincidence that these engineers tend to be voracious consumers of information, as being a student of the craft allows one to be better armed

with facts.
- They are willing to admit mistakes (see Skill #9: Own Your Mistakes), and to admit that they do not have all the "correct" answers. Their humility and lack of defensiveness is one of the most compelling reasons these engineers rise to the top, as working with them is much easier.

Exercises:
- The next time you want to make a strong argument, question whether you are attached to the outcome of the point, and why. Consider if you really have the facts on your side, and further, are there facts that you are not considering? Perhaps you are viewing things in a black-and-white manner, when the reality is not so disparate.
- Consider your team's views on the code they produce. Are the engineers personally attached to their code? Can you notice when this personal attachment arises within the team?
- If your team conducts code reviews, consider that process. Does the team understand that the code being reviewed is the property of the company, and not each individual? How might that realization affect how the code review is considered? Does your team welcome coding standards, or is this viewed with emotional disdain?
- If you find yourself having an emotional response to outside analysis of your ideas,

you should analyze yourself - are you strongly identified with your ideas? How are your actions perceived? Do your ideas define you, or are you really greater than your mental processes? Can you accept that the team might improve on anything a single individual could do?

Real-World Tale: Almost everyone falls into the trap of emotionally-driven thinking at one time or another. I have actually seen fisticuffs at a particularly contentious code review. People make non-fact-based decisions for a variety of reasons – personal bias, insecurity, ignorance, and so forth. With time and experience, one tends to see things in a deeper context, noticing that things are not really as black or white as what was once thought. Many technical decisions are not really "right" vs "wrong," they are simply valid for only a certain set of constraints – when those constraints change, the better technical decision may become something else. Similarly, decisions that businesses make are often made based on financial reality or networking and relationships and not on technical facts at all. Sometimes decisions are made based on entirely different criteria. For the working engineer dealing with operational decisions, it is most desirable that technical facts should drive the technical discussions. For strategic roles, other concerns can rightly enter the discussion. This is one reason why strategic thinking can initially be difficult for tactical thinkers.

On a related note, one of the side benefits of a formal peer review process and process standards (e.g. code reviews and coding standards in the software world) is that it reduces the notion of individual "ownership" of the artifacts being produced. Reducing the sense of ownership has the tendency to reduce personal emotion tied to individual contributions, focusing instead on the product itself. Another great reason to review the code produced by the team!

Skill #3: Question Assumptions!

Assumption is the mother of all evil in engineering. We assume that "If We Build It, They Will Come." We assume that the prototype will not be used in production. We assume that when a customer wants something with four wheels and a seat, they are asking for a riding lawn mower. There are many such daily analogies.

Part of the challenge is that written requirements are vague; language itself can be vague. There is no better illustration of this than a set of software requirements that produce an unsatisfactory result. You have probably heard the phrase "a picture is worth a thousand words." It is no accident that communicating in diagrams is often more revealing than anything that is spoken or written.

As an engineer, your duty is to seek out and remove assumption as much as possible. Don't automatically think that when a user says "real-time," they actually mean "500ms." "Real-time" might be more like "2s." You need not fear embarrassment from asking questions for which the answer may seem obvious. The benefit of ensuring clarity will far outweigh the danger of leaving assumptions on the table.

The struggle to address assumptions sounds

simple enough, right? The truth is - it is a deceptively difficult skill to master. To master it, you must strive to promote transparency on projects and sometimes across projects. You must be the person that is willing to draw a technical diagram in different ways, if it means illustrating a different point, design flaw, or possible problem. You must push for active voice instead of passive voice (Google it!) on your incoming requirements. You must be willing to clarify whether the words that one person is using mean the same thing as the different words that someone else is using to describe the same concept. Doing all this takes alertness and mental engagement in your topics! Improving this skill will not only make you better at your craft; you will notice these same skills applying to your life as well!

I found that when I started to improve in the art of recognizing assumptions, I started to notice them everywhere - on projects, in regular organizational behavior, in my personal relationships, and in my own habits. Only when you start recognizing the presence of assumptions, can you take action on exposing and addressing them.

Exercises:
- On your next project discussion, pay attention to the terminology others are using. Are there different words being used to represent the same concept? Ask both parties for clarification. You may encounter

meetings in which the participants are assuming that they are aligned around terminology, when in fact they are not - and nobody realizes it until you point it out.

- Ask questions about a seemingly obvious assumption on your project. As an example, here are a couple phrasings that I use:
  - "Perhaps this point is so obvious that everyone but me knows it, but I would like to ask if we have precisely defined what is meant by 'real-time'?...."
  - "I would like to validate my own assumption around the term 'real-time' – what do you consider real-time?...."
- Try a back-and-forth approach for exposing assumptions. This approach involves hearing the original context, then stating it back to the other involved party, to validate whether the point is truly understood: "If I understood you correctly, you are saying you think of 'real-time' as something around a second or two. Does it sound like we have the same understanding?"
- If you are writing design documents, try including diagrams. Explore standardized design notations such as UML and see if they can help you communicate with your audience. Does such notation help you communicate your ideas, or does it obfuscate your point?

Real-World Tale: The importance of questioning and clarifying assumption cannot be overstated. Once you become aware of it, you will realize how pervasive it is. For example, your product owner might assume that when a user selects the "email send" button, this is the precise moment when email is physically sent from your application; the engineers most likely assume that outbound emails are sent when they are actually sent to the SMTP server. Two technical teams that will integrate timestamp data might assume that they are using the one and only precise definition of a timestamp data structure, leaving the assumption on the table until it breaks during integration testing.

As another example, one of my groups once made a decision to hire a very bright fellow based on his stellar results from a programming test. His coding skill was amazing! He blew through our coding interview test in two different programming languages. However, in realistic conditions, what he actually coded was almost always unacceptable, because he would never ask questions or question assumptions from the intended users. Design documentation? Forget it. As an end result, we had to refactor almost everything he did on an ongoing basis. It was not a workable arrangement for very long. Don't be that guy. Ferret out as many assumptions as you can.

Skill #4: Be More Than A Coder

You probably already went to university, college, a technical program, or the school of hard knocks to hone your technical skills. You can probably pick up a new programming language in a couple days. Knowing more languages than anyone on your team is fun, right? Sure it is.

But are you really paying attention, past the mechanics? Past the semi-colons and the classes and the directory structures? Are you using your skills to the best ends, to ensure good results for the business?

You should become as interested in best practices, the general architecture of the product you are working on; the API that is presented to customers; how customers experience (or cannot experience) your user interface; how the product is tested; the development process that your team is using; what is working well, and what is not working well. If you take some time to appreciate and understand the entire craft, what goes into it, and what comes out of it, you will become more aware of the scope of what you are doing. Perhaps the activities of highest value are not where you are spending all your energy.

Exercises:
- There is a type of strategic analysis called a

"SWOT" (short for Strengths, Weaknesses, Opportunities, Threats.) You can find guidance and examples on the Internet. For this exercise, perform a SWOT on your own work environment. The point is not to do it perfectly; rather, the point is to get you thinking beyond the technical domain. This type of analysis is how management looks at the capabilities of your group. It is also commonly done when companies want to assess their own position relative to their competitors. This analysis might give you some insight that you are not currently considering.

- Based on your SWOT analysis, evaluate whether you are helping to address problems in your work environment. Do you see problems that call for your help? Are there opportunities that you could investigate further?
- If you are in an environment where you feel comfortable doing so, approach your immediate manager with your analysis and get his or her insight. You might learn some things about how management layers regard the challenges within your organization.

Real-World Tale: I once thought that coding itself was the primary value-add of a software engineer. I even reveled in a mild disdain for time spent on activities that were not somehow code-related. I was blind! Even the greatest codebase cannot save a software product if, for example, the user interface is lousy; or if the deployment model is wrong; or the product is too complicated to use; or it breaks in production. As engineering becomes increasingly global, the engineering and coding efforts are becoming a commodity. If you want to add value beyond the mechanics of the code that you and those forty other people on your team are doing, try developing the ability to look beyond the coding. I do a SWOT analysis, whether I am asked to or not, every time I go into a new position. It helps me gain perspective on my surroundings.

Skill #5: Build Speaking Skills

The ability to speak to people with a degree of ease and comfort is critical to a senior-level skill set. If this scares you, then consider this: it scares nearly everyone. There are fantastically brilliant engineers that completely suck at speaking in front of a group. Do you think it is easier to become brilliant, or easier to improve your skills at speaking in front of a group?

Given that the topic is scary for most, consider the opportunities that you will miss if you do not work on this skill. If you cannot effectively present your ideas, you are at risk of having someone else's worse ideas get implemented, simply because their ideas are packaged and communicated better than yours. Nearly everyone, myself included, gets nervous before speaking in public. But what is there to fear? You will probably not be beaten to death after you speak. So the fear is simply irrational, and related to perceived embarrassment more than anything else.

Here are some of the more important rules of speaking in public:
- Always face the audience! If you are using slides, this means you should never, ever face your slides with your back to the audience. If you have to read every word on your slides, then you are not prepared, and

there is a chance that your slides need work.

- Always try to speak in tones that reflect genuine interest in, or excitement about, the topic. Remember when you were in the audience watching a monotone speaker drone on and on? Don't be that speaker.

- If you naturally speak in quiet tones, start your presentation by asking people at the back if they can hear you. If your audience cannot hear you, then you might as well not be giving the presentation at all.

- Dress to match the expectations of your audience. That means wearing appropriate clothing for the situation. If you need help determining what "appropriate" is in the context of a presentation, ask a friend or a potential audience member for advice.

- Use open body language; for example, avoid crossing your arms in cultures where this is taken to be a defensive posture.

- Some presenters like to make periodic eye contact with certain people at different points of the room, and some presenters do not. You must study what you feel will work for you; but in any case, staring at the floor, or at your own slides, is not an option.

- Nearly everyone has nervous gestures that come out when they speak in public. Some people will automatically pace the floor; some people nervously fidget with a pen, a pointer, or a remote; some people have verbal habits that start to repeat themselves. You must study your own habits, and adapt those habits to what you can see in other successful speakers. This means either recording yourself, or practicing on audiences where you can safely get feedback on your presentation style.

- You must become a student of effective visual aids. Among other things, this means presenting relevant information in a consumable manner. This is heavily related to Skill #12: Adapt To Your Audience.

This is far from an all-encompassing list, but it will get you started. Your further study on this topic will be well worth your effort. Remember, the way to remove the fear associated with speaking is simply to practice it like any other skill. It **will** get easier.

Exercises:
- Sign up to give a talk about a topic you are comfortable with, to a friendly audience (e.g. your own team, a local toastmasters group, or your family.)
- Open up a talk with a friendly, relevant (and clean) joke – I give one in Skill #10: Be Interested In Others.
- Watch people who are very good public speakers, and note specifically what you think they do well. Did they use some specific techniques that held your interest? Did they do things that were not as effective? Did they display nervous behavior? Take the techniques that you thought were

effective and try them for yourself.

- Take a video of your presentation, then review the video and critique yourself. For this exercise, you must be cautious not to judge yourself too harshly. After all, the goal is to improve yourself! This can be a very humbling activity, but areas of improvement will usually be obvious, and improvements will pay off in your future presentations.

Real-World Tale: The best thing I ever did for my own speaking skills was to practice speaking to teams composed of my own colleagues. When I did this, I would have a friend in the audience who was taking note of any annoying speaking quirks. Once I was aware of my own peculiarities in speaking, I worked to fix them. Then I moved on to teams that were not as familiar, not as friendly, and so forth. When you handle your first hostile audience member, you will look back on your original fear and laugh about it. If you need help dealing with hostile audiences, the golden rule is: never get emotional or defensive. I invite you to study the topic further, since it is a very useful skill in every day confrontation.

When you improve your speaking skills, you will become a more effective presenter, and this will almost certainly be noticed by your management. This can open opportunities such as business-facing roles or customer-facing roles in your future.

Skill #6: Attitude Is Everything

You have probably heard somebody say that a positive attitude is a choice. Unfortunately, for many people, it is not a choice at all. They are on auto-pilot, acting and reacting to the world, without realizing that their behaviors influence those around them. They are unaware that they are living in a pattern, much less that the pattern can actually be changed.

The words that you choose have an effect on how you perceive and deal with the world, whether you realize it or not. I guarantee that it has an effect on your team, particularly if the words are hurtful, negative, or unnecessarily harsh. These words can also can affect your mind, your body, and your health.

The good news is that attitude is something that can be shaped with practice! One way to improve your attitude is by making a conscious effort to replace your negative words with more positive speech. By using positive speech, you can actually shape your own state of mind, and the way you interact with the world. Imagine you are at a code review with someone, and somebody makes the following statement to the author:

"That is a stupid idea."

Although the statement makes a point, it does not add much value. It also says something about the speaker's negative outlook. Compare it to this statement:

"I understand what you have done here, and I am glad we are looking at this together. I think we need to align the code with our design goals here <and so on…>. Let's improve this together."

This is arguably saying the same thing, but in a manner that is constructive and is far more respectful to the author. This is a more mature and professional way to offer your insight. With enough practice using this approach, you might find yourself being more supportive of the ideas of others, yet being able to shape the dialogue with the constructive nature of your insight.

If you have ever been stuck in a traffic jam, or in a long line of people at a store or in an airport, you may notice yourself becoming annoyed. Think about how illogical this is. Annoyed by the situation, by the reality of what "is." It is as though the world should conform to you and your needs, but it is somehow shocking or hurtful when it does not. Similarly to the traffic jam, charting your course in organizational settings will probably not happen in accordance with your own ideals of how it "should" happen. Becoming annoyed by this is simply our ego denying reality. It is important to analyze and check your own reactions. Annoyance at the reality in front of you is simply a recipe for a negative life, and it brings a constant set of negative outcomes. I encourage you to switch your perspective one hundred and eighty degrees. Where you see challenges, appreciate the fact that with these challenges comes opportunity. That traffic jam is an opportunity to practice being content with your state of mind. The line at the airport is an opportunity to notice that you are there with your family, or that you can engage in a conversation. The challenge of having to sell your idea several times over before anyone pays attention is really an opportunity to improve your own sales pitch ability, or perhaps to open new channels for selling other ideas.

Exercises:
- Listen to the words that others use. Notice that some people use powerless speech, such as "I have to...." or "It makes me...." and see if you can determine a correlation between their powerless speech and their actual physical condition. For example, someone who uses the phrase "it makes me sick" might be frequently ill. Someone who says "get off my back" may have actual back or posture problems.
- Practice substituting positive words for negative words in your own speech. For example, instead of referring to someone as "stupid," call them "under-skilled" instead; they might need help in the form of your skills!

- Practice substituting expressions of your own power, rather than powerless expressions. For example, instead of saying "I have to...." say instead "I choose to..." By doing so, you are convincing yourself that you are taking responsibility for your own path.
- A "mantra" is a word or phrase that is repeated. Mantras are frequently used in areas of life such as meditation, competitive sports, or any situation where a particular behavior is needed to produce a certain result. Mantras can be effective as a tool to help counter negative self-dialogue. If you find that your internal dialogue is very negative to yourself, you can write down some explicit mantras to counter your negative messaging. I have actually recorded my own, and I use this recording as an uplifting personal dialogue to exercise a positive outlook.

*Real-World Tale: An experienced salesperson once told me: "Attitude is everything." I had no idea what he meant, until I explored the Buddhist concept of "right speech." This is a life changer, if you explore the topic deeply. I learned how my own negative thoughts and words affected my beliefs, my outlook on life, and the morale of my teams. Once I began to speak more kindly, I found that I also began to **think** more kindly. I was able to move away from my own negative behaviors, toward a positive, loving, creative life. I greatly improved my enthusiasm for the craft of building* *software. Choosing negative words, actions, and behaviors just takes up energy that could be spent on better things. This is what people really mean when they tell you that positive attitude is "choice." Doing your work with a positive attitude will bring you better professional relationships and more professional opportunities.*

Skill #7: Lead Or Follow

In almost every organization, there are leaders, followers, and managers. Although some companies are unique, leading and managing are generally two very different skill sets.

A manager is more focused on day-to-day task and time management The manager may or may not be closely involved with project details. On the other hand, a leader is not necessarily a manager; this is a person that inspires and motivates others. Leaders are normally found on the front lines of the engineering activities, which is why it is said that "leadership is from the front." To use a typical office analogy, a leader is not afraid to get up to the whiteboard and possibly risk their own ego position in order to validate assumptions so that the technical direction is better understood.

It is rare that actual "leaders" are in the top ranks of larger companies, although there are exceptions. This is part of the natural evolution of companies from small size (more leaders at the front, to push the company to initial success) to large size (relying more on managing the operations of the already-established business.) On any particular project, the actual "leader" role might vary among a variety of people.   For example, one person might be a leader of the payment functionality, and another might be a leader of the database group.

Chances are, you already know who the leaders are in your team and in the teams around you. They are the go-to people who know the problem space, know the technical solution, and are able to clearly enunciate their domain. Some of those leaders take high accountability for their product, and others do not. Some leaders are more effective than others in certain situations. You should explore your own leadership skills enough to understand your own limits. This starts with recognizing where there is a void of leadership, or where there is a problem that is in need of a solution, and using the skills presented in this book.

Exercises:
- Look around your group. Can you identify the managers, leaders, and followers? Do you think a good leader makes a good follower?
- Study one of the people who seem to be a leader in your organization. What makes him or her an effective leader?
- Try to identify an area of your service or product that is not well understood, and study it. Become the person that can enunciate it effectively. Just through your improved domain knowledge, you may become the de facto leader for that area, and explore your leadership skills. Expect this to

be difficult and uncomfortable at first - if it were comfortable, everyone would do it. Discomfort, in this case, means that you are expanding your own boundaries.

- When you recognize that there are areas that are devoid of leadership, volunteer to lead them. You may be successful or you may be unsuccessful, but either way you will learn things that you would not have learned otherwise.

Real-World Tale: Books have been written on this topic alone, so it invites your further study. The point here is to understand that these roles can vary widely based on the maturity and culture of the company, and the dynamics of the organization (see Skill #17: Understand Organizational Dynamics.) As an example, I was once given the opportunity to lead a large project, where the previous leader was not achieving project goals. The previous leader had a very contentious interpersonal style that was causing conflict at almost all levels, and tended to ignore the details of the product functionality itself. Since I was much more adept at some of the skills in this book (in this case, Skill #6: Attitude Is Everything and Skill #21: Know Your Product), I was able to push the project past the obstacles that caused him difficulty. If the organization were more conflict-driven, perhaps the outcome would have been different.

Ideally, you should decide whether you want to

be a leader, manager, or follower in your career. If you move toward one role, you might have to give up on the other two, to some degree. For example, if you move into management, your technical skills will erode, which will make it more difficult to return to a technical role in either the leader or follower capacity. So when you take a role that is outside your preference, consider it carefully and with your future in mind.

Skill #8: Don't Hit Send

Part of effective corporate behavior is making good choices about how to communicate, when to communicate, and which tools are effective. Believe it or not, email can sometimes be dangerous. This sounds like a trivial concern, but at some point you may be exposed to a situation where you must exercise restraint. This can be a very difficult skill to master, particularly if you are working in an intense environment.

There are two scenarios that are worth exploring:

Sending Emotional Emails
Repeat after me - **never, ever** send an emotional, reactive, or rude email to anyone in a corporate environment. Period! Don't hit send, even if it is a response to another person that was terribly rude to you. Always take time to clear your head: take a walk, relax, or talk to a friend. Consider whether you even want to respond. You can always write the response and send it to a friend, or let it sit around in your drafts folder. Ideally, you should work out out differences directly, personally, and behind closed doors as much as possible. Email is easy to misinterpret, and the email can be saved forever, to be used against you later.

Ignoring Proper Communication Channels

As you become more senior in your career, you will be increasingly aware that organizational structure is usually in place for good reasons. The obvious example is sales and development. The sales organization has a set of goals around selling the product or service. They are heavily dependent on the product roadmap and delivery dates, which is information that is often carefully messaged by the project managers, product managers, and so on. This careful messaging is necessary to ensure that proper expectations are set between engineering/development, the product management teams, sales, marketing, and ultimately the customer. Development staff, particularly in a large company, may be many steps removed from those communications, so it is very easy to assume that this communication channel does not exist. As an engineer, you are in a position to know the gory details of the product or service, and your interpretation of those details can be understood very differently by the sales organization.

Imagine sending a terse email about something as tactical as a broken build to the entire sales force. They might think the product is in chaos! Would they be as excited to sell the product if they knew what was really happening behind the scenes? The point here is that you must be cautious when communicating across organizational bounds, particularly in email due to its persistent nature. You should involve your product management colleagues for any communication that involves the outward-facing part of the business. If you are ever in doubt about whether it is appropriate to communicate across the organization, ask a colleague, your manager, or your project manager for help. Even then, ask for help in crafting the specifics of the message. When faced with this scenario, I will usually use phrasing like this: "I'd like to ensure that we message this appropriately. Can you proofread this for me? I would really appreciate your help."

By now you can see that email is somewhat like a power tool - very effective, but it can hurt you if used without caution.

Exercises:
- When somebody really upsets you through email, avoid responding via email. Instead of reacting in anger, go out of your way to be even more kind to them in the future. You might find that positive and friendly behavior can disarm them, and also lightens the way you feel about the situation. Getting upset or reacting emotionally only gives the other person control over the situation. Remember that angry or rude behavior usually says more about the person from which it emanates.
- Look at how your management structure or your product management makes announcements about your product or service. Look at the language that is used;

look at the colleagues who are receiving the message. If there is terminology included that you don't understand, ask for help in understanding why it is communicated that way. This is a useful method for learning the communication protocols at your company.

Real-World Tale: A former manager of mine used to say: "Cool your jets! Use my 24-hour rule – forget it for 24 hours, and think about your response tomorrow." That is one of the best pieces of advice I ever received. In every case where I ignored that advice - which was not very often - I regretted it later. The truth is, people can be fired because of nasty emails. Avoid engaging in negative correspondence.

In regards to the use of proper communication channels, let me just say that I learned that lesson by making that very mistake. I would rather save you from the experience!

Skill #9: Own Your Mistakes

The ability to admit mistakes is one of the most significant characteristics that separates amateurs from professionals.

For this discussion, let us assume that we are dealing with an engineering environment, where mistakes are not usually the result of malevolent actions. They are usually the result of high complexity, lack of oversight, miscommunications between teams, and so forth.

When faced with a mistake, there are two basic approaches that can be taken:
1. Accept the mistake, correct it, and move forward, or
2. Blame someone else

If you are wondering about how professionals handle such a scenario, the answer is number one!

It is often easier to point fingers at someone else. You can see this behavior often in government and corporate organizations. Sometimes you see it directly in interpersonal behavior. Blaming behavior leads to an environment where people try to hide mistakes, cover things up, and promote distrust. Let's face it, nobody wants to work in an environment where finger-pointing is condoned. Admitting to the mistake is called "taking accountability." Yes, it might feel terrible when it happens; this is normal and expected. It is the more difficult and challenging path to take, but also far more personally rewarding. So when a mistake appears on your doorstep, own it and fix it! Bonus marks if you can ensure that it never happens again! There is nothing wrong with doing some root cause analysis to figure out what happened, but this should be done positively, without throwing colleagues under busses. Remember, what goes around, comes around. The person you throw under a bus today, could be your boss next week.

With most mistakes, bugs, or problems, there is an opportunity to contribute skills, make new friends, forge new connections, and help your organization succeed. But there are times when the path to take is not so clear. Taking accountability does not mean that you must be a willing martyr in the face of problems. If a situation arises where there is tremendous risk to you or your organization, discuss it with your manager, your mentor (see Skill #16: Get A Mentor, Be A Mentor), or your team. For example, if your manager's manager's manager commits to a very visible deliverable based on your analysis, and you later discover an error in your analysis, you should discuss it immediately with your manager and be willing to contribute a solution. Your manager may see that there are ways to resolve the problem that do not require high-level strategic adjustment, and thus would prevent unnecessary embarrassment to your high-level leadership.

Exercise: Look at how mistakes are handled in your company. Is there a culture of blame? Or is there a culture of accountability? Is it a culture that claims to promote accountable behavior, but in reality is anything but? How can you help improve that?

Real-World Tale: I once received this advice from a university adviser: "Never admit that you don't know something. Go and study it, and come back with the answer." Thankfully, I realized that this advice seemed fundamentally flawed. Here is how I handle such a scenario today:

Them: "What is the correct answer to this hypothetical situation?"
Me: "Honestly, I do not know the correct answer, and I would rather give you the correct answer than the incorrect answer. I would like to study the problem further and present a strategy to you. How does that sound?"

This is an example of taking ownership of my own limits and working to come up with a solution. Similarly, I have made mistakes that I worked hard to clean up afterward. In one case, I changed some code that disabled some important (and costly) downstream activities. I could have blamed the existing code, but at the end of the day, the code and some of the systemic issues around it just had to get fixed. So I owned up, apologized, and fixed both the original problem and the problem I introduced.

Owning one's limits and admitting to mistakes is the mark of individual responsibility. If you receive advice like, "Never admit that you don't know something" or "Never admit to being wrong," you should consider the source with suspicion. If you cannot deal constructively with mistakes, there will come a time when there will be nobody to blame but yourself, and you will pay for it with your reputation and your hard-earned respect among your peers. You don't want to be that person.

Part II: Your Professional Relationships

Skill #10: Be Interested In Others

An old software joke goes:

Q: What is the difference between an introverted software engineer and an extroverted software engineer?
A: The extroverted software engineer stares at **your** shoes when he talks to you.

There are plenty of engineers who forsake positive interactions with other people, with the perspective that the code or the technical product (and associated technical skills) are all that matters. We have all had this bias at one time or another. But this perspective is always self-limiting because sooner or later, in software or in life, you will have to work with others. If you do not prepare for this, you may experience sub-optimal results!

Even if you are an introverted personality type, it will help your career if you can learn how to engage someone in conversation.

The great part? There is an easy way to do it. Take a lesson from Dale Carnegie's legendary "How to Win Friends & Influence People": the easy way to start a conversation with someone is to **ask them to talk about themselves**. Learn their name. Treat this exercise like an engineering project, where you are eliciting requirements from someone.   Ask questions about that person, about their likes and dislikes.   Listen to them.   Hear the words that they choose, the situation they are in. Put yourself in their position and contemplate it before returning to your world.

Exercises:
- Particularly on a day when you are feeling anti-social, go out of your way to engage someone in conversation.   Don't cut the conversation short because you have to get back to coding. Watch what happens when you ask questions. See their reaction when they talk about their kids. Are you realizing the power of this interaction?   With this simple approach, you will make connections that can take you far further than your coding skills alone.   Added bonus: you might make a new friend.
- Go to a technical recruiting event and speak to a recruiter. Technical recruiters are well-versed in conversations with engineers, and they present interesting fodder for conversation. The side benefit is that you will gain a better understanding of your local job market.
- Interview at other companies. This is a great way to keep your interpersonal skills on point, and it will also illustrate whether or not your technical skills are up to date. Interviewing does not mean you must take the job!

Real-World Tale: The ability to engage in conversation is critical to your social skills, both on and off the job. I am more introvert than extrovert, so I had to practice this skill extensively. Many years later, I still actively use similar practices in interview situations, discussions with customers, discussions with other engineers, and even on stage as a musician. Like any other skill, it becomes easier with repeated practice.

Skill #11: Practice Building Trust

Trust is what makes people want to work with you. When you make a commitment to someone, you should try hard to fulfill it. Delivering on your commitments and following up on your tasks are essential to being regarded highly by your peers and your management.

That said, there are also some direct interpersonal skills that will help you build trust quickly:

- Be honest in your dealings with others; it helps to use what you practiced in Skill #2: Reason From Facts.
- Making eye contact during conversation will immediately make you more credible and likable in interactions with people.
- The most important word in any language is the name of the person with whom you are speaking. Using their name in conversation is a sign of respect and recognition. Have you ever met a person that seems to remember everyone's name? You were probably impressed by that – which means it had an impact!
- People tend to enjoy interacting with people who they believe like them. If you are trying to build trust with "Person A," how can you make Person A think that you like, respect, or admire them? You would not just directly

say "I like you," because this would be strange and artificial. One way to achieve this is to pay attention to your organization (Skill #17: Understand Organizational Dynamics) and let Person B (whom you happen to know is friends with Person A) know that you respect Person A. When Person A hears this from Person B, you might be pleasantly surprised that your dealings with Person A get much easier. This is an example of using savvy interpersonal skills to affect a working relationship toward a positive goal. This will work most effectively if you are genuine in your opinion of Person A.

- When you are in a position to place blame on another person or group, even if blame is warranted, try to approach it from a supportive point of view. Perhaps that other person or group needs your help. Perhaps the root cause is something systemic that should be addressed. If you place blame, you can easily make a new enemy and shut down the cooperative channel that might have existed there. Remember, you might need help from that other person or group someday!

Exercises:
- Find a way to attend a sales presentation from your company's top sales people. Watch how they interact with prospects or customers. Notice how they present the

value proposition. Take what you think are their effective techniques, and try them yourself.

- Go shopping at a local car dealer. Compare the behavior of the car salesman with the behavior of your company's sales people. Do you notice a difference in the professionalism and the approach? If you are an engineer working for a car dealer, you can skip this one!
- Try practicing eye contact on your own reflection in a mirror. Talk about any topic for a minute, and look yourself in the eye five times in that minute. It should not be a stare-down!
- Try to use someone's name in every conversation you have with that person.
- To practice your follow-up skills, take one week and keep a log (see Skill #15: Value Others' Time And Expertise) of your own action items. Make sure you follow up on each and every one within the following week. Do your colleagues appreciate it? Does it feel different to have a systemic follow up practice?

Real-World Tale: Building trust is a cornerstone of establishing and evolving your credibility within your team and within a broader organization. There are many techniques that you can study to build this skill. One source you can study is great sales people. Sales people have to master these skills quickly, and the great ones are an invaluable resource in learning how to connect with people. Whenever I can join a sales call, particularly when I know that the speakers are very skilled, you can bet that I will be taking notes on the techniques that I think I can use.

If you are genuine in your intentions, studying and practicing different approaches will increase your trust-building skills. As your skills increase in this area, you will be able to sell your ideas more effectively, and you will be better at networking across groups. It is also very useful in dealing with management layers.

Skill #12: Adapt To Your Audience

Engineers are very intelligent, and sometimes we feel like we need to let the world know how smart we really are. We make up acronyms that nobody else understands and use overly obtuse terminology with some degree of pride. If left unchecked, we can explain solutions from the highest level of detail, to the lowest level, covering everything in between. In certain audiences, this behavior leads to adverse outcomes. Skill #5: Build Speaking Skills already pointed out that effective speaking is very important. Additionally, what you speak about - and how you say it - is just as important.

Identifying proper content is vital to being an effective communicator. This involves two key components: knowing your audience, and tailoring your content to information that is relevant and consumable for that audience. This often means taking a complex topic and expressing it in simple form by removing details that do not add direct value to the audience. To illustrate the point, consider this example. You are a software architect at an enterprise software company. You are responsible for implementing single sign-on across some different applications which have historically caused end-user pain by forcing multiple logins. To solve the problem, you made some great decisions including the choice of a solid third-party authentication system. You are presenting a summary of the solution to an internal business audience at the company. Imagine these two scenarios:

Scenario 1: The Amateur

You present a detailed technical explanation of the original problem, including a breakdown of how sessions are managed and how user data is stored. Then, you give an overview of the trade-offs involved in the selection of the authentication system (you are rightly proud of that decision, and therefore everyone should follow your discussion to the same conclusion.) Then, you give a detailed overview of that authentication system, followed by a demonstration of the application interface of that authentication system, and the details of how it integrates with the existing applications. Finally, you give a demonstration of how it all works. You also put pictures of your children on each slide, because they are the cutest children anywhere. Your presentation exceeds your time slot by twenty minutes, because there were a lot of details to cover.

Scenario 2: The Professional

Before the presentation, you take few moments to study the list of attendees. You discover that the audience is completely non-technical people. You call one of your non-technical friends on the business side and do a dry-run of your presentation with him/her, to fine-tune your approach. You create some speaker evaluation cards asking the audience to review specific areas where you know you are a weak presenter. When the presentation time arrives, you mention that you are working to become a better presenter, and that you would appreciate if the audience would help by filling out an evaluation card at the end. You start with an agenda which only has two items on it: a demo, and a short discussion of the solution approach. You give a live demonstration of a user logging in twice before the change, and a live demonstration of a user logging in once afterward, pointing out the seamless transition between applications. Then, you give a high-level overview of the technical ramifications or maintenance implications of the overall solution, followed by a ten minute question/answer session. If anyone wants low-level technical details, you invite them to meet directly in a separate detailed session. You complete the presentation on time, because you brought a friend from your team with you, who kept track of your time spent presenting each topic.

These scenarios are extreme opposites to illustrate a point. Scenario 1 might work for a presentation to the architect's own immediate team, but it is probably ineffective for business users who neither understand, nor care about the technical details. The presenter in Scenario 2 did the homework, adapted to the situation, asked for and received help from colleagues, and engaged the audience. The attendees from the presentation in Scenario 2 were probably impressed with the demonstration, and further impressed that the presenter was engaged enough to ask for feedback; that means the architect just received visibility and credibility from an audience outside the technical realm! This person appears to be on the way to becoming a great presenter, and will likely be asked to interact across teams more often. You can see that in Scenario 2, the architect put aside his/her natural pride in the technical decision making, and focused on what was most important to the audience. This is a difficult thing to do for a any technically-oriented person.

In adapting to your audience, there is no "right" or "wrong" approach, there is only the degree to which your ideas are effectively communicated. In the scenarios above, you should strive to be the Scenario 2 presenter, by working to understand your surroundings and engaging with your colleagues.

Exercises:
- When you are in discussions with technical colleagues, try this experiment. When there is a pause in the conversation at the end of a thought or statement, extend the pause without talking. Just be silent. The idea is to see what the other person does with the space in the pause. Your colleagues might frequently try to fill the pause with technical talk or other banter.   Now you can understand why filtering content down to only the important details can be very challenging; there can be a lot to say, and a

tendency to say all of it.

- Try to explain your current project to a non-technical person. Can they understand it? Could they draw a picture of it? Or do you get mired in the details?
- Watch other people present information to an audience. Was the information tailored to you, or was it confusing? Why do you think that happened? Did the presenter distract the audience by including irrelevant content?
- Watch people whom you think are effective presenters or communicators. What are they doing that makes them effective? Take their approaches and tailor them to your style.

Real-World Tale: The ability to express a complex topic and express it in a form that is consumable to an audience is a key skill possessed by high-level engineers. But it rarely comes naturally. As you can see from the scenarios above, it requires you to mentally detach from the topic and re-evaluate it from the perspective of the consumer of the information. Different people do this in different ways, but it is not magic. All you need is some help from your audience. For example, as an extremely visual person, I know that if I can understand a topic enough to draw some diagrams of the important points, then I can generally extract the most relevant information and get the point across. So I may draw design diagrams in one, two, three or more different ways and have a colleague from my target audience examine it, to see if they can understand the point I am trying to communicate. I may start at standard UML and end up with stick figures and boxes; after all, the point is not to invest ego in one's UML skills, it is to communicate an idea. The side benefit: in drawing the diagrams, I am also mentally exploring the associated concepts and improving my own understanding of the domain. It's a win-win!

With some practice, you can become become adept at tailoring your communication to your audience. Coupled with Skill #5: Build Speaking Skills, your ability to interact across various groups will automatically improve. Your network will expand, and you might even be exposed to other career paths that you had not previously considered.

Skill #13: Handle Criticism Professionally

Have you ever been to a restaurant and ordered a meal, only to have it be disappointing? Did you stay silent when asked how the meal was? How can the chef correct the problem if nobody says anything?

Criticism is almost always difficult to hear. When someone criticizes you, take note of it without reacting. If the criticism is incendiary or accusatory, you will want to consider it deeply before reacting (see Skill #8: Don't Hit Send.) But if the criticism appears to be given with good intentions, you should take some time to do some serious self-analysis. If you determine that the criticism seems warranted, you should seriously consider altering your behavior or approach. Remember, this person has taken the time and energy to give you a thoughtful review. Your gratitude might even be in order. You may find it helpful to ask a friend if they observe the same behavior in you; if your friend agrees with the person giving the criticism, then it is usually indicative of something real that you need to improve.

When asked, give criticism in an honest manner. There is some debate about whether criticism is best given in a public or private setting – there are pros and cons either way. My personal experience has led me to the approach of giving praise in public, but to offer direct criticism behind the scenes, particularly if the situation is significant or embarrassing. It almost always helps to give specific examples of problem behaviors that you observe. For example, if I observe a colleague becoming very negative in their interactions with the team, I will write down the observation (this is much easier if you are taking notes, as mentioned in Skill #15: Value Others' Time And Expertise!) and have a private conversation with the individual: "Joe, I noticed that since mid-June, you have seemed really disappointed with our team; what's going on?" It is important to clear the air so that working relationships stay productive. When faced with more significant situations or harassment scenarios, get your human resources representative involved and don't try to solve it alone.

When it comes to formal criticism, as in performance reviews, I recommend using suggestions for improvement rather than personal commentary: "Joe struggled a bit with SQL performance this year, I recommend that we bring in training on database query optimization."

Handling criticism is part of life in the corporate world, so you need to have a strategy to deal with it. Look at it as an opportunity for growth. Taking feedback to heart and acting on it is how real self-improvement is done!

Exercises:
- Find a colleague you are on good terms with, and take him or her out to lunch. Ask him or her if there is something you can do to improve your working relationship with that person.
- For a more difficult exercise, do the same thing with a colleague with whom the terms are not as good. You may be interested in what you learn.
- Even more interesting, take your manager to lunch, and ask him or her if there is anything you could be doing better. I recommend taking notes if you do this (see Skill #15: Value Others' Time And Expertise.)

Real-World Tale: Dealing with criticism can be one of the more difficult aspects of corporate environments. Having been a people manager, I have dealt with criticism in multiple directions. I personally enjoy 360-degree feedback programs, because I am interested in knowing how I am perceived by my team members. This allows me to adjust my own behavior like the chef in the restaurant. It has been my experience that managers who are not interested in collecting feedback on their own skills are missing major opportunities to become more effective at their craft. As individual contributors, we should respect our colleagues enough to give constructive and honest feedback, but also to give honest evaluation to the feedback that is received. In Skill #6: Attitude Is Everything, I mentioned that there are many people who are on auto-pilot, and this is commonly the case with the use of feedback. Don't be the one on auto-pilot.

Skill #14: Manage Perception

We don't like to admit this, but people will treat us according to their perceptions. Our appearance, the words we choose, the way we hold our posture – these things will certainly have an impact on how we are perceived.

The reality is that you are a salesperson, in the sense that you will eventually be selling your ideas and opinions to others. Particularly if you interact with non-engineering groups, being mindful of your perceived appearance is important. Why not use every advantage?

Here are some specific techniques for managing how you are perceived:

- Use professional language. If you are in an environment where your peers use street slang, then do what you need to survive. But you must realize that you will have to adapt to professional language when management is involved.
- Clothes matter. Yes, your clothes can shape how you are perceived, particularly when you interact with non-engineering groups.
- Posture counts. If you have a natural slouch like I do, you should try to overcome it. It can be perceived as depressed or disinterested body language.
- Get in shape. It's an odd statement on

society, but physically fit people are perceived differently. I would advise you to do this most importantly for your own health; but the side benefit is that you might enjoy a more positive perception on a professional basis.

Exercise: When you have a few hours to kill during the week, put on the ratty jeans, geek t-shirt and baseball hat that you normally wear to work, and go to an upper-crust store in a downtown area. Then do it again another day, wearing professional attire. See any difference in how you are treated?

Real-World Tale: At some point, you may find yourself being someone's manager. When this happens, as it happened for me, you will start to look at your surroundings very differently. As an easy example, imagine that you are a manager, and you are about to meet with a customer. You have to take a technical person into the meeting with you, and your two top engineers are these people:

- *Engineer A: the life of the party on the team, always wears a rock and roll t-shirt and a baseball hat, known for blunt language*
- *Engineer B: not quite as much the partier, usually wears a polo shirt; decent hygiene, uses complete sentences*

Would you put Engineer A in front of one of your customers? How about one of your investors? It's an easy decision. You can see how Engineer A is very likely getting passed over, even though he or she might be the world's best coder, or a great person with whom to have a few beers. If you intend to move to higher-level roles, you will need to understand how perception shapes decisions.

Skill #15: Value Others' Time And Expertise

Top professionals value their own time, and also the time of others.

This is expressed in some key ways:
- In conversation, don't interrupt the other person.
- Take notes when someone is giving you valuable information that you can use. Nothing says "I'm not paying attention" like asking the same question, forgetting the answer, and asking again.
- When you facilitate meetings, make them effective! That means following basic meeting effectiveness skills, such as:
  - Don't have meetings unless they are necessary
  - Start meetings on time, and end on time
  - Every meeting should have an agenda with a clear purpose
  - Nominate a person who will take notes (also known as meeting "minutes") in the meeting, and will send the notes to attendees afterwards
  - Review action items from any prior meetings about the same topic
  - Assign action items and track these in

the meeting notes
- Keep the meeting on track
- Exhibit a willingness to schedule your time around others.

Exercise: Look up "meeting effectiveness" on the Internet. You will notice many of the same points above. Try injecting some of these points into your meetings and notice which are most valuable for your organization.

Real-World Tale: The Value of Keeping a Notebook

I was working for a defense company right out of university. One day, a senior engineer from my team took me aside and said: "Do yourself a favor and keep a log book. Put the date on the left and your notes on the right, for each day. We're on a military project and you might need your notes some day. Then you are going to thank me for this advice."

Initially, I thought he might be spewing nonsense, but I humored him. I got a nice engineering log book, and started jotting out my notes, some component level designs, and so forth. Every page had a date on it. Sure enough, about two months later, I had to justify part of the software design to our military customer. If I did not have my design notes, I would have seriously regretted it.

Staying out of trouble was strong motivation,

but I noticed two other benefits that I had not considered:

1. I could remember things better, because I made a stronger mental connection to the topics I had written.

2. I found that people with whom I met considered me to be more respectful of their time, simply because I was taking notes! I think this is analogous to a restaurant server who writes down your order - you would expect that if they wrote down your order, it would be more likely to be correctly served. This practice had the effect of building trust with my colleagues.

To this day, I still carry a notebook. I can tell you what I was working on, on this day, five years ago, or ten years ago. When I present technical topics to my colleagues, I can immediately tell who is interested, and who is not – by who is taking notes. I encourage every software person and every engineer to engage in this practice. It works.

Real-World Tale: The Rubber Duck Effect
I was once in a situation where an organization was composed of very strong personality types who constantly interrupted each other at meetings. It was very chaotic and abrasive, bordering on toxic. I decided to try something different. I went to a toy store and bought a rubber duck, which I then brought in to the meetings. In each meeting, I set the expectation that the person holding the rubber duck was the only one allowed to speak. In

order to have a discussion, the duck would be passed - or thrown - from speaker to speaker. This protocol had exactly the effect that I was after. The exclusive-speaking rule seemed to instill some awareness about interrupting one another, and the ridiculousness of passing a rubber duck around seemed to lighten up the entire atmosphere. The interrupting habits decreased, and meetings became much lighter, relative to what they had been. I still have the duck.

Skill #16: Get A Mentor, Be A Mentor

It is easy to forget this, but most highly successful people have had multiple mentors along the way. There are a variety of reasons to have a mentor:
- Helping understand and work through challenges in an organization
- Networking with the mentor's contacts by building relationships through the mentor
- Pure self-improvement

As your career grows, you may find yourself losing your direction, or encountering plateaus in your development. A mentor can help and challenge you to overcome these things. Mentors need not be in the same line of work, department, or company. Some people have several mentors, for the different areas of their lives that require work. Whatever the scenario, what matters is that there is something in the mentoring relationship that helps you along your path.

Seeking a Mentor
If you decide to seek out a mentor, you must be cautious to ensure that the mentor is someone who can actually teach you. This seems self-evident, but it can be more difficult than it appears. The mentor must be someone you would like to emulate to some degree for their own accomplishments. For example, if you are training for the world weightlifting championships, you are

probably not going to take much advice from the trainer at the local gym - you would seek out someone who is at your level, and preferably beyond. A suitable mentor should have the time and ability to help you. The top software engineer on the planet might be a poor mentor choice if they have no time to speak with you. I recommend writing down your objectives in a mentoring relationship, and considering these things to be criteria by which you gauge whether you are learning from that relationship.

A good mentoring relationship usually consists of regular meetings (either remote or in person) and some degree of follow-up on both sides. Ideally, a good mentor is like an honest friend. You will engage in two-way conversation; your mentor will listen to your dilemmas, discuss your ideas, but also challenge you when you are making questionable assumptions or bad decisions. A mentor is not there to give you affirmation! You must prepare to hear feedback that might not always be exactly what you expected. Different mentors can take different approaches, and it may not always be obvious that you are deriving value from your mentoring relationship - so you must be mindful of your original goals and re-evaluate every so often.

You can usually tell when you are in a questionable mentoring relationship if one of these things is happening:
- Your mentor is ignoring you or appears to be

uninvolved
- Your mentor is too busy for you, or not openly communicating with you
- Your mentor violates your trust or does not hold your conversations in confidence
- Your mentor agrees with everything you are doing
- Your mentor disagrees with everything you are doing

If you see these signs, you should either discuss it openly with your mentor and resolve it, or be prepared to move on from that relationship.

Being a Mentor
There is no finer moment than seeing someone reach their own success, having played some small part in that success. As you progress in your own career, you may be approached to become someone's mentor. This is a high compliment, but should be approached with maturity and respect, as it can be both rewarding and risky. Imagine mentoring a person that is so reckless, that the relationship itself becomes embarrassing to you as the mentor. As much as person being mentored must carefully consider their goals, the mentor also has a responsibility to establish their own parameters regarding their inclination to mentor someone, and the boundaries of that relationship. This requires time, commitment, and mental engagement for the mentor. In addition, a mentor must be cautious not to violate the trust of the person under their guidance, or serious

interpersonal damage can result.

In any mentoring relationship, it is best to have a very open discourse on both sides, right from the start. This allows both people to express expectations, boundaries, and so forth. In general I would highly recommend mentorship, as it can help you learn and progress further than you could without such a relationship.

Exercise: Without actually approaching anyone about it, think about who in your career you would want as a mentor, and why. Would Bill Gates be a good mentor? What about Mark Zuckerberg? Why?

Real-World Tale: I was once in a mentoring relationship that was set up by a politically-oriented manager, mostly to get information from me about another manager in the organization to whom I happened to report. If left unchecked, I might have been in the middle of a political battle and probably suffered ill will from both sides. To make a long story short, once I realized what was happening, I adjusted my own position, and eventually removed myself from the situation. This experience taught me what a destructive mentoring relationship was like.

One the other hand, I was lucky to have some great role models from whom I still borrow on a daily basis. They called me out on my negative behaviors, challenged my beliefs, and made me more aware of my own path. Being a mentor to others allowed me to help my colleagues to adjust their own paths, and to make positive changes in their careers. The proudest moments of my software career have been due to acting as a mentor to my colleagues.

A mentor can change your entire career path for the better, or it can be a negative experience, so this is something to be approached with care.

Part III: Your Organization

Skill #17: Respect Other Roles

It is natural for an engineer to think of the technical product or service as the center of his or her universe. However, the core offerings are invariably a piece of a larger picture. You can develop the best back end, and the world's greatest user experience, but no users arrive to use it. The truth is, other areas of expertise are needed in order to reach a successful outcome. Marketing has to generate and groom a pipeline full of leads; sales has to turn those leads into sales and revenue; product management has to translate the market needs into requirements; support has to make sure existing customers are happy; the quality organization has to make sure the releases minimize regression; management has to keep all of these roles operating together. You can see that these roles all have their own goals, for very valid reasons.

Sometimes, the goals of other roles are orthogonal to the goals of engineering and development. For example, it is normal and expected that sales, marketing, and product management will ask for more functionality than engineering can deliver. It is expected that engineering will evaluate the incoming direction and determine what is feasible and achievable. It is also expected that quality teams can and should push back on engineering in the face of risk, regression, or bugs. The best organizations realize that these roles have natural friction, and they simply make the decision to operate together, trusting each other to make sound decisions, and moving ahead. When one role gets out of balance versus another, the result can be very negative. If the product management side is not doing its job, then the wrong thing might be built; if the engineering side ignores feasibility, infeasible things will be attempted; if the quality function is not present, regression will almost certainly enter the system. As an engineer, you have an obligation to support the business direction, but also to help the business understand when the direction carries danger to its own ends. This is where you can and should apply your skill set in communicating risks, and possible alternative approaches.

The point here is to accept the fact that as an engineer, you have an ecosystem of important roles around you. Once you are conscious of this, you might realize that there is plenty to learn from those other roles, and that learning from them can lead you to different areas in your career. As an example, if you have practiced your speaking skills (Skill #5: Build Speaking Skills) you may start to develop a network of colleagues in the product management or sales organizations. Many companies have technical roles that exist to support sales with operational demos, prototypes, integration support, and so forth. It is not uncommon for these roles to be filled by former members of the engineering staff who happen to possess customer-facing skills.

Exercises:
- Find a top sales person in your company and buy him or her lunch. Ask them what a day in their life is like. You might find that the perspective of a sales role is very different from that of an engineering role.
- Try to help your product owner or product manager the next time they need technical assistance with communicating technical details. It will be educational for you to understand what information actually matters to other audiences.

Real-World Tale: Everybody in the organization is relying on each other for their success, and it is the mark of a good team player to seek out opportunities to understand and consider this when making decisions. If you can be empathetic to the challenges of the roles around you, you will be in a position to contribute your skills in different ways. The more you interact with these other roles, the easier it will be to function with comfort between the different facets of your company. This will in turn give you a more visible presence and an increase ability to impact change.

A person who influenced my career once gave me a different perspective on the natural give-and-take of the business-engineering interchange. I think of it as the "qualified-yes" approach, where the engineer gives a positive answer with a qualification caveat, rather than saying "no." For example, assume that a business colleague asks: "That replicated database is very expensive. Can we eliminate that?"

Me: "I get the impression that you have a cost reduction target in mind, is that true?"
Business colleague: "Yes, about <xyz> dollars per year."
My answer:"Yes, we could eliminate the replicated database; but the risk is that all of our customer data can be irretrievably lost if the database drops. I don't want to live with that possibility, do you?" (This was the qualified-yes.)
Business colleague: "No, I suppose not...."
Me: "Alright then, I strongly recommend we keep that replicated database. We might get close to your target if we did our load balancing in software; how about this idea....<and so on>"

I could have simply answered "no" with some technical jargon, which might have shut down the conversation. But by attempting to understand the problem and employing a more positive tone, it is easier to have a constructive discussion with business colleagues while balancing the needs of the engineering side.

Skill #18: Understand Organizational Dynamics

Understanding your organization is critical to being an effective player in a corporate environment. Think about it: if your boss carries a lot of influence in the organization, his or her position will help you. But what if your boss is in a weak position within the organization? What if you need to sell your ideas to a different part of the business in order to get traction? You should pay attention to the structure and how it operates.

When you start looking at the organization from the perspective of achieving your goals, rather than as an obstacle, you might realize that there is a myriad of complexity and opportunity:

- Are there powerful decision makers in your reporting line? This might mean that your management structure has strong input into the overall direction.
- If powerful decision makers are not in your reporting line, then where are they, and how can you influence them?
- Does development report to a C-level executive? This would mean the development organization formally aligns with the business at only the highest level.
- Who influences whom between your management reporting line and the business

reporting line?
- How are major decisions really made?
- Does Sales run the company, or does R&D have political power?

If you start engaging with people in other roles within your company (Skill #17: Respect Other Roles), you will start understanding organizational characteristics like those above. You will build your own network, and have an informal team of contacts that you can use to get perspective, work on opportunities, and possibly help influence organizational change. This is what is meant by navigating the organizational structure.

Exercises:
- Get an organizational chart for your company. Compare your reporting line to others. Think about which people are the most powerful, and which people have the most influence. Who would you approach if you had an idea that you wanted to act on?
- Try to make some friends outside your team by using some communication skills (see Skill #10: Be Interested In Others.)

Real-World Tale: I was blissfully ignorant of corporate dynamics for many years. I viewed organizational politics as an obstacle to making progress. But in retrospect, that is because I was ignorant of how to relate to it. It is important to be open to organizational politics. It is a fact of corporate life - your goal should not be to escape it, but rather, to put it to positive and ethical use.

In 2011, I used basic organizational awareness skills to spearhead a project that was eventually demonstrated by the CEO of one of the largest enterprise software companies in the world. I did it in a six-month time frame, from an isolated office that was otherwise totally insignificant within the company. This had nothing to do with my technical prowess. It was all about finding out who to talk to, working with other teams, knowing what to deliver, and how to deliver it.

There are many strategies and nuances here that cannot be covered in a small amount of text. A great start is to read the book "Political Savvy: Systematic Approaches to Leadership Behind the Scenes" by Joel R. DeLuca. This book is the original basis for the exercise on this skill. After reading this book, I never looked at corporate politics the same way again. This is something you should consider deeply.

Skill #19: Support The Business Direction

Every line of code and every design decision carries an element of change and possible risk. Therefore, when you can detect that certain outcomes will constitute significant effects the trajectory of your group, product, or service, you should consider the decision relative to the type of company that is around you.

As an example, a company that is more strongly driven by their business side will generally operate in a coin-operated manner: incoming revenue will trump engineering more often than not. This can manifest itself in the presence of "silo" development, where products or services are created for each business domain, with little regard to long-term engineering processes that might make subsequent iterations less painful. On the other hand, companies that are strongly engineering driven will tend to pay attention to engineering practice, and will have strong holistic processes - sometimes at the expense of modern technology or rapid development velocity. It is an interesting statement on organizational behavior that one can often observe the organizational structure of a company by the organization of the product, service, or system that it produces. This phenomenon is known as "Conway's Law."

By striving to understand your company's operating culture, you can make decisions that account for it. When a company is very sales-centric, there is little point in being upset with the sales force for driving large functional changes into the product; that is their role! It also pays your salary! Instead of looking at the situation negatively, try to shape it by making the best decisions you can in considering the holistic environment. You could form a grassroots architecture group; meet with the technical leads and promote best practices together; jointly address assumptions in your APIs; step in to help your product owner communicate the right technical message to your sales colleagues. If you and enough of your fellow engineers do this, it is entirely possible to offset short-term decision making with solid technical decisions that offer payback in the future. If you are in a very engineering-driven company, you can encourage fresh technology thinking by starting up a volunteer hackathon; exploring bleeding-edge technology and reporting on it to your peers; making pitches to management that there are ways to speed up your development cycle while mitigating risk.

As an engineer, you have an obligation to support the business direction, but also to help the business understand when the direction carries danger to its own ends. This is where you can and should apply your skill set in communicating risks, and possible alternative approaches.

Exercises:

- The next time you get a new requirement, ask yourself what level of risk it carries, and how you might go about mitigating that risk. Try having that conversation with your business team. You may learn completely new assumptions in the ensuing discussion, and possible alternate designs can appear.
- Does your company care about best practices? Why or why not? Is there an association between lack of best practices and what you can perceive as the business goals?
- Look up Conway's Law. Can you think of a company where you might be able to observe this?

Real-World Tale: A mentor once told me: "As long as you are making the best decisions you can for the business, you are never going to be far off the target." While I am sure there are limitations to that statement, the advice still guides my thinking on a daily basis. I find great value in attending business-side discussions that most of the technical staff do not attend. How else would a person understand the long-term direction?

Skill #20: Talk To Customers

It is not uncommon for developers and engineers to be several steps removed from the viewpoint of "real" customers. This is reflected in the cold speech of software requirements: "User shall <do this>," "As an Administrator, I want to <do that>." It becomes easy to lose sight of why you are creating software - and more importantly, for whom. Compare the steps that an actual customer communication must travel through to reach the engineer, in a large company versus a small company:

Small Startup Company
- Customer submits feature request on web form
- Form contents mailed to business person
- Business person talks to engineer because they are sitting next to each other
- Engineer gets requirements, starts building

Large Company
- Business management team meets with customer management team
- UX team meets with different members of customer team
- Business team meets with different members of customer team, elicits requirements
- Requirements sit on the shelf for two months
- Business team balances those requirements

against sales, marketing, other requirements
- Requirements sit on the shelf for two months
- Requirements massaged by business, sales, marketing
- 100% turnover of original UX team, new UX team gathers requirements again
- Two months later, engineer gets requirements, starts building

You can see that a large company has a very different set of challenges to deal with. As the customer's original requirement passes through each layer of organization, the original intent is changed, colored in terms of the bias of each group, magnified, expanded, diluted, and so on. Sometimes there is very good reason for this, such as to balance the requirement of one customer against competing requirements from hundreds or thousands of others. As a result, it can be very enlightening to hear the direct feedback in the words of the customer. In some cases, you can determine erroneous or missing requirements, because the sharpness of the customer's communication has become obfuscated by requirements analysis.

If you know what your users really think, you are in a better position to objectively discuss your product with your product team. As a result, you may start to understand requirements differently, and even adopt slightly different designs, given that you are more aware of the user's assumptions.

Exercises:

- Ask yourself if you could use the product you are building. Why or why not? Should you act to change some things?
- If your company follows user-centered design processes, ask if you can participate.
- If your company tracks customer-facing metrics like Net Promoter Score, try to listen to some of the customer feedback.
- Go to a shareholder meeting or a user conference.
- Talk to someone who actually uses your product. You don't have to act on all feedback, but it will give you a dose of reality, and possibly some good material to discuss with your product team.

Real-World Tale: I cannot count the number of times that hearing the customer's words directly has led to a great discussion with my product management colleagues. Having this perspective can foster a clearer, more engaged discussion. One of the most rewarding things you can do as an engineer is to solve a direct customer pain point. If you take up an effort to solve a customer-facing problem, you should remember to keep your product management team aligned in your activity, because you will need their help and support to deliver the solution. Remember from Skill #17: Respect Other Roles, it is not a one-person show.

Skill #21: Know Your Product

For large or complex products or services, it is very easy for an engineer to develop sharply compartmentalized knowledge of the overall solution. But as much as you should know the inputs and outputs of your own subsystems, it is also important to be aware of other subsystems, whether they are directly dependent or not.

Large companies often employ engineers called "architects" or "system engineers" who are responsible for a holistic, cross-functional perspective. Even with these roles, success at a holistic level is not guaranteed. In the absence of such roles, the responsibility of the individual engineers to be able to consider system-level issues becomes even more pronounced.

By understanding your system-level architecture, you will inevitably make better system-level decisions. For example, if you know that your enterprise messaging system will support a throughput of a certain rate, and you are aware that this rate is higher than the consuming system two steps downstream from you, then you can (and should) reach out to your architecture group and the owner of the consuming system and put your assumptions to a discussion and resolution. This is the approach taken by senior level engineers. It is vastly better than watching the system blow up in production!   In addition, by being proactive in approaching the solution, you gain the confidence, trust, and visibility of your system engineering colleagues.   This is an example where taking accountability will produce positive results.

If you build your understanding of the product functionality, you can similarly have more meaningful discussions with your product management colleagues.   The more you are familiar with the product, the more you will be exposed to product-level discussions.   For example, if the product team suggests that the user be made to re-enter a piece of information that is already in the browser session, you can make the case to leave the redundant entry out. There would be no way for the business team to know that information. Thus, you can see that understanding the product can result in a less painful user experience and possibly a quick win for everyone involved.

Exercises:
- Pair up with a QA person to help test parts of the application with which you are unfamiliar.
- If your company follows a user-centric design process, try to see it in action.
- Pair with your development operations (usually known as dev-ops) group to understand the deployment/release process. You might get some credibility with the dev-ops team for caring enough to understand it.

Real-World Tale: This should be self-evident, but it is an often ignored point. If you don't know the product, you are completely unarmed for discussion, and you are doing the business side a disservice because they often need your technical knowledge of the product in order to make smarter decisions. This does not mean you must be the technical expert across all functional areas - you just need to know how to get the technical answers and work with other people. If you have built up your network using the other skills in this book, this is much easier because you can use your network to bring in expertise or help in areas with which you are less familiar. Knowing where you need to get support and bringing that support into a discussion is not a sign of weakness. It is the mark of a professional. I have often done this on larger projects where I was in unfamiliar territory. I will bring a relevant technical colleague in and introduce him or her using something like the phrase: "This specific area is not my core competency, so I have asked my colleague <name> from <area of expertise> to help us with this conversation."

What Comes Next?

You alone are the key to your own success. There is no "right" or "wrong" approach; there are only the results you get, and how you apply yourself. If you put this book down and forget that you read any of it, then nothing will change. If you expect your career to evolve to great things simply by being at your desk writing top-quality code, you should get ready for disappointment. You must take charge of your own path, as much as you can given your particular situation. You will have to explore your own boundaries, and in some cases, push against them.

I want you to start using these skills. I suggest that you start with one or two skills in each category and work on them for a certain period of time. For example, you might want to make April the "speaking skills" month. If you are feeling very motivated, work on one part of each skill for a couple weeks, until you have acted on something in every area. After a year, you might be a completely changed engineer.

I hope this material will offer insight that helps you (and keeps you out of trouble) throughout your career. Some of these skills take years to master. Think of it as a marathon and not a sprint.

If you find that some of these skills serve you

well, I ask that one day you share your experiences and skills with those around you. In this manner, as we improve ourselves, we can also improve our industry and the world around us.

Real-World Tale: The Iron Ring

In a tradition dating back to 1922, many engineers graduating from Canadian engineering institutions receive a ring called "The Iron Ring". The Iron Ring is a symbol of the obligations and ethical standards associated with the engineering profession. The Iron Ring is worn on the little finger of the dominant hand, where the ring's facets are noticeably felt while the engineer is working. This in turn reminds the engineer of his or her obligations. The ring symbolizes the pride which engineers have in their profession, while simultaneously reminding them of their humility and their high standards of conduct.

When a newly-trained engineer receives The Iron Ring, the ring's facets are rough, even sharp. As an engineer progresses through his or her career, the edges are worn smooth. Your software career will likely follow a similar transition. Expect that there will be hard lessons along the way, but it is these lessons that will shape you into your final form. It will not always be comfortable, but it will definitely be worth the effort.

(Part of this content was paraphrased from an associated Wikipedia article)

About The Author

Cory Berg graduated with a degree in Computer Engineering in 1993 at age 21, and has been developing software professionally ever since.

At one time or another, Cory has been a skier, a weightlifter, a swimmer, a hockey player, a comedian, and a bar guitar player. With the rest of his time, he enjoys spending time with family and friends, coding, motorcycling, guitar playing, meditation, and improving his writing skills.

Cory can be reached via Twitter @codepoppa or via email at cory.berg@softwareplusplus.com.

If you would like to be a part of Cory's further work on related topics, please visit http://www.softwareplusplus.com.

www.ingramcontent.com/pod-product-compliance
Lightning Source LLC
Chambersburg PA
CBHW061014050326
40689CB00012B/2642